MARINE BIOLOGISTS

Robin Koontz

Educational Media

rourkeeducationalmedia.com

Before Reading:

Building Academic Vocabulary and Background Knowledge

Before reading a book, it is important to tap into what your child or students already know about the topic. This will help them develop their vocabulary, increase their reading comprehension, and make connections across the curriculum.

1. Look at the cover of the book. What will this book be about?
2. What do you already know about the topic?
3. Let's study the Table of Contents. What will you learn about in the book's chapters?
4. What would you like to learn about this topic? Do you think you might learn about it from this book? Why or why not?
5. Use a reading journal to write about your knowledge of this topic. Record what you already know about the topic and what you hope to learn about the topic.
6. Read the book.
7. In your reading journal, record what you learned about the topic and your response to the book.
8. After reading the book complete the activities below.

Content Area Vocabulary
Read the list. What do these words mean?

acoustic
atmosphere
bioactive
conservation
ecosystems
estuaries
hydroelectric
oceanography
organisms
spawn
tributaries
watershed

After Reading:

Comprehension and Extension Activity

After reading the book, work on the following questions with your child or students in order to check their level of reading comprehension and content mastery.

1. Where do marine biologists work? (Summarize)
2. Why is it important to teach people about conservation? (Infer)
3. Explain the keystone species idea. (Summarize)
4. How does tourism affect marine life? (Asking questions)
5. How has the work of the biologists featured in the book contributed to the field of marine biology? (Summarize)

Extension Activity

Oil-based products, like plastic bags, have a direct effect on marine wildlife. Do you know what products you and your family use that are oil-based? Create a list of oil-based products that you use. How can you reduce the amount of oil-based products you use each day?

TABLE OF CONTENTS

A HELPING HAND

Imagine strolling along a moonlit beach, the sky filled with stars. Suddenly you see a dinosaur lumbering out of the sea. With extraordinary concentration, she uses her flippers to dig a massive nest in the sand.

This is how marine biologist Jose Urteaga describes a leatherback turtle arriving to lay eggs on the shore. Jose works in Nicaragua, Central America. The area is home to five of the world's seven sea turtle species. Nearly all of the turtle species are threatened. The leatherback turtle is critically endangered.

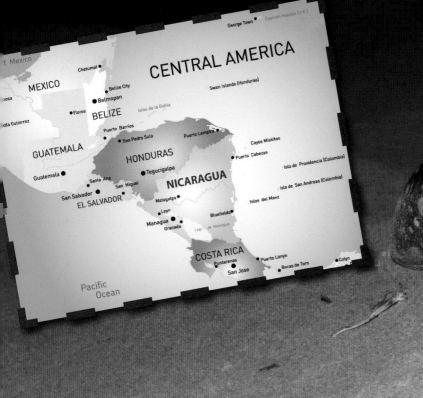

Leatherback Sea Turtle

Jose and his team watch the 1,000-pound, 6.5-foot-long (450-kilogram, 2-meter-long) turtle as she slowly scrapes in the sand. They know that when she is satisfied with the nest she is digging, she will lay her eggs. The team is ready. When the eggs start to come, they catch the eggs with a plastic bag. The eggs will be taken to an area that is safe from poachers. Sometimes they are taken to a special hatchery set up for the turtles.

Female leatherback turtles lay a clutch of 80 to 85 fertile eggs. They might nest several times in one spring-summer season. The hatchlings emerge during the night, 55 to 75 days later.

Jose's sea turtle **conservation** program on the Pacific coast is a combination of everything from science lessons to puppet shows. Jose attempts to discourage people from poaching precious turtle eggs. He also patrols all the nesting beaches to protect the endangered creatures.

Thanks to Jose's work, more than 90 percent of leatherback turtle nests on the Pacific coast are protected. Before the project started, nearly every egg laid was taken to sell for food.

An animal is considered critically endangered when it is facing an extremely high risk of extinction in the wild in the immediate future. Marine biologists are often involved in research and conservation of threatened and endangered marine animals and plants.

All sea turtles found in US waters are listed under the Endangered Species Act (ESA). Source: NOAA

green turtle

hawksbill turtle

Kemp's ridley turtle

leatherback turtle

loggerhead turtle

olive ridley turtle

Goldring-Gund Marine Biology Station in Las Baulas National Park in Costa Rica is also in Central America. It is run by The Leatherback Trust (TLT), an organization devoted to saving sea turtles, especially leatherbacks. As many as 24 researchers at the station work together to study and help nesting turtles. They also host students from middle and secondary schools in field-based learning programs.

Research teams measure the sizes of turtles as they return from the sea to lay eggs. Many of the turtles have satellite tags that track their movements.

How does satellite turtle tracking work?

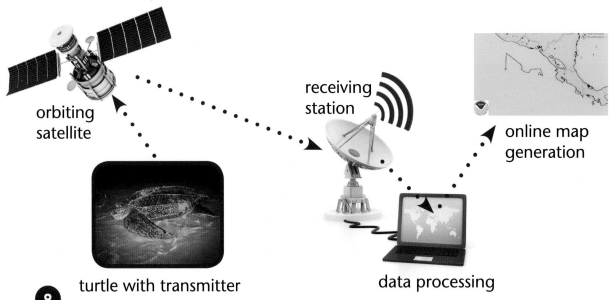

orbiting satellite

receiving station

online map generation

turtle with transmitter

data processing

The tags were implanted when the turtles were first hatched or found on the beach. The tag data tells scientists how far the turtles travel in search of their favorite food, jellyfish. The scientists can even find out how fast the turtles swim and how deep they dive! The tags also tell about environmental hazards that might hurt the turtles.

The lion's mane jellyfish is the world's largest jellyfish. It is a favorite food of leatherback turtles. The turtle snags the jellyfish with its pointed lip. Backward-pointing spines in the turtle's mouth and throat trap the prey as it is gulped down.

If the turtles survive long enough, the females will return to the place where they were born to lay their eggs. Researchers will monitor their nesting sites, too. They will count the eggs and record the temperature of the nests. If they are worried that the eggs won't survive, they might move them to special hatcheries.

Who are these sea turtle heroes? Many of the research scientists who work hard to protect the world's sea turtle population are marine biologists.

Leatherback hatchlings are two to three inches (50-75 centimeters) long and weigh about two ounces (50 grams). If they survive, they can grow to be more than six feet (1.8 meters) long and weigh up to 2,000 pounds (900 kilograms).

Many factors caused sea turtles to become endangered. They survived millions of years, and then humans appeared. Longline and driftnet fishing, developments along the coast, artificial light, egg poaching, pollution and collisions with watercraft have all contributed to the demise of one of the Earth's oldest living creatures. Nature reserves led by marine biologists and other scientists are set up in nesting areas to try to stop and reverse the decline in sea turtle populations.

A sea turtle could mistake a plastic bag in the water for a jellyfish. Eating the plastic can cause digestive problems and possible exposure to toxins.

WHAT IS A MARINE BIOLOGIST?

A marine biologist is immersed in a watery world. Marine biology is a branch of **oceanography**. Marine biologists study every kind of sea creature, from whales to microscopic **organisms**. They observe how the creatures behave and how they connect with the environment. They study where they live and where they sleep, if they sleep. They observe what the creatures eat and study that, too.

Many marine biologists study the health of coastal **ecosystems**. They monitor the impact of pollution as well as environmental and man-made disasters. One example is the Deepwater Horizon disaster in 2010. Marine biologists were called in to assess the damage from the massive amount of spilled heavy crude oil, which gushed into the Gulf of Mexico and polluted wetlands in the area.

Gulf of Mexico

Two NASA satellites captured time-lapse images of the oil spill, which began April 20, 2010, following the explosion of the Deepwater Horizon oil rig.

Poseidon was not only god of the sea, people believed he was able to make the Earth shake with his trident, causing earthquakes.

People have always been in awe of the mysterious sea. In Greek mythology, the oceans were a strange world filled with gods and sea monsters ruled over by King Poseidon and Queen Amphitrite.

Aristotle was a Greek scientist and philosopher, born in 384 BCE. He was the first person known to record marine life. Aristotle identified different species and studied how they lived and reproduced. Many people call Aristotle the father of marine biology.

Aristotle
384 BCE - 322 BCE

Captain James Cook is also known for his descriptions of plants and animals that lived in the sea. Cook was the first to record all the amazing things he saw in the oceans around the world. A few decades later, a famous scientist named Charles Darwin became known for his studies of marine biology as he researched evolution.

Charles Darwin
1809-1882

Captain James Cook
1728-1779

Still later, thousands of marine specimens were gathered during the voyage of the HMS Challenger in the 1850s. Zoologist Sir Charles Wyville Thomson was the lead scientist on board. He and his crew traveled throughout the world's oceans. Their research became the basis for the study of marine biology at that time and for many years. It was also the first time that ocean explorers had the equipment to explore deeper than anyone before them.

After that, more and more explorations took place. People began setting up laboratories just to study marine life.

Today, marine biologists can be found working in all kinds of places. They might be wading in a creek, paddling in a swamp, or diving off a research vessel. They could be photographing beautiful coral reefs, exploring the deep sea while inside a submersible vehicle, or taking water samples from a tide pool. Marine biologists also work on computers and in labs. They may write research papers or teach students.

A marine biologist is an important contributor to the medical industry. They study microorganisms from the sea, searching for new **bioactive** compounds. Bioactive compounds, such as antibiotics, enzymes, and vitamins, are things that have an effect on humans and other living creatures.

Marine biology can be a commercial venture as well. Marine biologists help engineers design better dams that protect spawning fish. Others manage fish hatcheries or study the travels of migrating fish, such as salmon.

Fish ladder structures are installed to allow migrating fish to travel around dams or spillways that otherwise would block their migratory route.

The Delta submersible is a three-person vehicle that can dive 1,200 feet (365 meters). Since it was first manufactured in 1987, it has performed over 6,400 dives.

What marine biologists all have in common is that they work with marine organisms, whether their work involves getting wet or not. And all marine biologists have the same goals. They observe, learn from, manage, and often help protect marine life and water systems of all sizes.

Otis Barton and his partner, William Beebe, stand with the first bathysphere. William is wearing the homemade diving helmet he created in 1925.

Otis Barton invented the bathysphere, the first submersible vehicle able to dive deeper than 3,000 feet (914 meters) into the ocean. The bathysphere made its first dives in 1930. Until his invention, almost nothing was known about the deep sea. A few years later, he invented a Benthoscope. It could dive up to 4,500 feet (1,372 meters)! The submersible research vessels used today can go much deeper, but they use many of the same design principles as the original bathysphere.

MAD AS A MARINE BIOLOGIST!

As a marine biologist, Samantha Craven is especially interested in protecting the fragile ecosystems of the marine world. The 7,109 islands that make up the Philippines have a diverse range of both aquatic and land-dwelling creatures. The coral reefs there and throughout the world are facing new challenges. Pollution, climate change, and destructive fishing methods threaten the health of fragile coral reefs. This is where Samantha focuses much of her work. She dives, takes amazing photographs and videos, and spreads her excitement about marine biology to teach and encourage others about the importance of conserving our oceans and coral reefs.

Samantha was 11 years old when she decided she wanted to become a marine biologist. She and her family spent their holidays in the Philippines, where she loved diving in the clear, blue-green water, exploring the colorful coral reefs.

The coral triangle around the Philippines has more kinds of fish and corals than any other marine environment in the world.

After college, she worked in conservation, teaching students about tropical ecosystems. Samantha knew that she wanted to focus on conservation. She began working to protect coral reefs in the Philippines.

CHINA

TAIWAN

Luzon Strait

South China Sea

Babuyan Islands

Aparri

Sagada

San Fernando

Banaue

Philippine Sea

Baguio

Luzon

Quezon City

PHILIPPINES

MANILA

Tagaytay

Legazpi

Mindoro

Samar

Panay

Iloilo

Bacolod

Leyte

Palawan

Cebu

Puerto Princesa

Negros

Bohol

Sulu Sea

Mindanao

Davao City

Zamboanga City

Jolo

Basilan Island

MALAYSIA

INDONESIA

Celebes Sea

One of her jobs was Principal Investigator of the Oslob Whale Shark Research project in the Philippines. In Oslob, feeding whale sharks is a tourist attraction. Sam and her team studied the effects of the practice of encouraging these threatened animals to depend on humans for food. Some of the negative effects they noted were that the sharks became less afraid of boats. They were often injured by their propellers. There was also concern about their nutritional needs. The sharks were being fed just one kind of frozen food. Another problem was the sharks were often not learning how to feed themselves in the wild.

Whale sharks are the largest fish in the sea. Luckily, their favorite food is microscopic plankton.

Sam learned that sometimes scientists had to do more than practice their craft. In conservation projects such as the whale shark feeding investigation, she had to be a good communicator and a teacher. The world of marine biology is bigger than you'd think!

In 2014, Sam was still involved in the conservation world, working hard to protect our marine ecosystems. One of her jobs is to teach divers about responsible diving practices.

Sam has advice for young people who are interested in marine biology: "Get as much experience as you can before, during, and after college ... working or volunteering for surveys in the field, in a lab, in an education center, whatever you can find, will teach you skills that University cannot."

Sam's blog is called "*Mad as a Marine Biologist.*" She posts photos, videos, information, and stories about the strange and beautiful creatures in her undersea world. She keeps people informed about her exciting activities. Sam hopes her readers will learn to care about the marine world as much as she does.

The Great Barrier Reef in Australia includes more than 3,000 individual reef systems. It is the only living thing that can be seen from outer space.

Coral reefs only cover a tiny fraction of the Earth's surface, yet they support possibly one quarter of all ocean species. These species depend on the reefs for food and shelter. Coral reefs are the most diverse of any other marine ecosystem. And they are valuable to people. The reef systems provide food, shoreline protection, and jobs.

HANGING OUT WITH OTTERS

Michelle Staedler has been a friend to sea otters since 1986. As a marine biologist, she is involved with the Sea Otter Recovery Plan and helps with new policies about sea otter conservation. California sea otters have been listed as threatened under the Endangered Species Act since 1977.

THREATENED

In her efforts to help the animals, Michelle studies what sea otters eat and how they raise their pups. Michelle will often follow the same otters for a period of time.

Michelle uses a VHF (very high frequency) radio receiver to locate a study animal. The otters she observes are outfitted with radio transmitters so they can be located and studied more easily.

Sea otter researchers Michelle Staedler, left, of Monterey Bay Aquarium and Tim Tinker of the USGS locate sea otters to study their diet and behavior.

Michelle says this research involves spying on a mother otter, "Watching her every move and timing each motion." She uses a grid in a logbook to record lots of detailed information about the mother otter's behavior and activity. Using a stopwatch, she carefully times how long the otter dives. She writes down what and how much food the animal brings back with her. She notes how long it takes for the mother to eat. Michelle even has a system of measuring the food based on paw size. Something as big as three paws gets a number three. She watches to see if the mother otter shares her fare and if her little pup accepts the food. Michelle also records when the mother shows her pup how to use tools to eat.

Sea otters often use a rock to open a clam shell. They smash the clam against the rock until it cracks. They also use a rock to pry food from rocks underwater.

Linear Density
otters per 500 m coast

0

5

10

Point San Pedro

Pigeon Pt.

Santa Cruz
Monterey Bay
Elkhorn Slough

Monterey   Seaside

Pt. Sur

Ragged Pt.
San Simeon Pt.   Cambria

Cayucos
Morro Bay

Pismo Beach

Ventura County

Santa Barbara County

Pt. Conception   Santa Barbara

Gaviota State Park   Pt. Rincon

San Nicolas Island

Washington
Oregon   Mont.
Idaho
California   Nevada   Utah
Arizona

0   25   50   100 Kilometers

This map shows the number of sea otters in their California range. Researchers have been studying the otter's population recovery since the animals nearly became extinct in the 19th century.

Otters seem to vary in what they eat. If a mother otter teaches her pup to eat something that is abundant, such as clams, it might have a better chance of survival. An otter that prefers more unusual food might pass that information along to her pup. Marine biologists believe that this could give the baby a tougher life, and could be a reason for the decline in sea otter populations. Other factors such as pollution also affect their numbers.

The data that Michelle collects helps scientists understand more about the behavior of otters. The information will hopefully help in their recovery and conservation. These scientists all know that sea otters are part of the Earth's valuable ecosystems.

Otters have to eat a lot to stay warm because unlike most marine mammals, they have no blubber to insulate their bodies. They spend most of the day diving for food and eating.

Biologists consider sea otters to be a keystone species. A zoologist named Robert T. Paine first introduced the keystone species concept. A keystone species is an organism that can seriously affect the ecosystem if they are gone. When sea otters were nearly killed off for their fur, there weren't many left to control the population of the creatures that they ate. These otter food species, such as sea urchins, eat massive amounts of kelp. Without otters, their overpopulation nearly destroyed the kelp forest. That loss had an adverse effect on other marine life. Once sea otters were protected from hunting and their numbers returned to areas such as the California coast, the associated marine life was slowly restored.

kelp

purple sea urchin

A HISTORICAL RESCUE PROJECT

The Elwha River is on the Olympic Peninsula in Washington. The river empties into the Strait of Juan de Fuca. Long ago, it was a very productive salmon stream. Salmon mature out in the ocean, but they breed, nest, and hatch in freshwater rivers and streams.

Strait of Juan de Fuca

Elwha River

Olympic Peninsula

Washington

Mouth of the Elwha River

STRAIT OF JUAN DE FUCA

The Elwha River is a 45 mile (72 kilometer) river on the Olympic Peninsula in Washington State. It flows generally north to the Strait of Juan de Fuca. The river is one of the few in the Pacific Northwest with all five species of native Pacific salmon: chinook, coho, chum, sockeye, and pink salmon.

In the early 1900s, two **hydroelectric** dams were built on the river. Salmon and other migrating fish were blocked from traveling up the river to **spawn**. Plus, the large reservoirs created by the dams changed the **watershed**.

The US federal government began removing the Elwha Dam September 2011. By March 2012, the Elwha River could flow freely through the site.

Recently, the two dams were removed and their huge reservoirs were drained. At the time, in 2011, it was the largest dam removal in US history. The goal was to restore the river and its entire watershed to a natural state. Now, instead of being trapped in the lower five miles, salmon and other fish species are free to travel upstream more than 70 miles.

They are also free to travel up **estuaries** that flow into the river. The historical spawning habitat is protected by the Olympic National Park. Marine biologists are hoping that the river restoration project brings salmon and steelhead numbers back to their historic pre-dam levels, along with other members of the ecosystem. Many of these native fish are threatened or endangered.

A female chinook salmon makes a nest inside Olympic National Park. These fish were among the first to recolonize waters that hadn't had salmon in 100 years.

USGS divers establish a transect to measure the species diversity of kelp, algae, invertebrates, and fish found near the mouth of the Elwha River. A transect is a path for counting and recording species.

Anne Shaffer is a marine biologist who is studying some of the effects of removing the dams. During the time that the dams spanned the river, sandy deposits called sediment collected behind them. For more than a hundred years, millions of cubic yards of sediment amassed. Releasing the tons of sediment was done carefully and slowly. Too much at once could upset fish migration. The dam removal project was even stopped during the spring and fall migration periods.

The released sediment immediately began to reshape the river and change the shorelines. Biologists estimate that it could take decades to see the full effect of the dramatic but welcome change to the river and its **tributaries.**

A USGS hydrologic technician operates a sediment-sampling reel at the Elwha River in Washington. River sediment was sampled during the dam-removal project to monitor the amount and timing of sediment released.

The cloudy waters of the Elwha River and the coastal waters of the Strait de Fuca mix directly offshore of the river mouth. The sediment from the river forms a large coastal plume.

Anne and her team are studying the area where the river meets the saltwater tides. These places are called nearshore areas. The regions used to contain very little sediment. Now a new ecosystem is forming that hasn't been there in more than a hundred years.

Anne and her team are busy trying to figure out what kinds of marine life are moving into the restored haven. They also want to study the effects of the new sediment coming in. They are hopeful that some particular fish are spawning, or nesting, in the fine grain sediment. The tiny fish, called smelt, are a favorite food for young salmon.

The scientists trudge year-round through the water and sandy deposits, scooping up bags of sand. They test the sand in the lab, searching for eggs and other signs that the tiny fish have been nesting. In areas where sand has built up, they have found evidence of surf smelt.

They also spotted another kind of smelt that was once a main source of food for coastal tribes. This smelt, called a eulachon, is listed as threatened under the Endangered Species Act. It had not been seen for many years. While the team was focusing on the marine shoreline for nesting sites, seeing these fish in the estuary was an exciting discovery!

Smelts are fished commercially and for recreation. People fry the little fish and eat them whole, bones and all.

A marine biologist records information during an Elwha River snorkel survey. The surveys are done to monitor the fish coming into the area.

Anne and her team also count fish along the marine shoreline. Counting fish is not easy, but it's important. For one thing, it tells the scientists how fish species are reacting to the large sediment loads released by the dam removals. Biologists predict that as the habitats restore, there will be an abundance of fish again.

FIELD NOTES

Counting fish is no easy task for marine biologists. Anne's team uses a beach seine, or net, that is laid out in a divided-off area of the nearshore. A frame cradles the net so that they can identify, count, and measure the captured fish. The fish are only out of the water for a brief time.

A WHALE OF AN ADVENTURE

Susan Parks is an assistant professor of biology at Syracuse University in New York. She and other researchers study the ways that humpback whales locate food. It turns out these whales have a few tricks up their flippers.

Susan specializes in **acoustic** communication. She was part of a project that spent more than 10 years monitoring the whale's feeding behaviors. The work was done off the coast of Massachusetts. They tagged the whales with special recording devices that could work underwater. This way Susan and her team could study the sounds whales make as they search the seafloor for food. They hoped to discover some links between the unique sounds they make and their feeding activity.

One thing the team discovered was that the whales make "tick-tock" noises if they hunted in a group during the night. The sounds were like clocks ticking in the pitch-black water. Perhaps the sounds spooked their prey. The whales typically preyed on eel-like fish called sand lance that buried themselves in the ocean floor. When the fish popped up, the whales could snatch them up and eat them. But the researchers also noticed that the whales did not make the sound when they hunted alone.

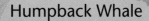
Humpback Whale

The sand lance burrows into the sand at night to avoid being eaten. They also lay their eggs in the sand. The eggs are so tiny that they look a lot like grains of sand.

Instead, they were silent. It seemed that the whale sounds were alerting others in the group that they'd found something good to eat. It was like a dinner bell!

The sounds also seemed to alert nearby whales. There were clues that the other whales overheard the sounds and came to the area to join the dinner party.

Marine biologists have studied humpback and other whale vocalizations since they were first recognized in 1967. That was when marine scientists Roger Payne and Scott McVay discovered that humpback whales sing. A single whale produced a series of sounds sometimes for as long as 30 minutes. Then it repeated the same series exactly the same way, often for several hours without pausing. At the time, the scientists had no idea what the songs meant, or if they were sung by male, female, or both genders.

But they did discover that each individual whale sings its own song. Roger produced a record album in 1970 called *Songs of the Humpback Whale*. The recording helped to change the way people saw the animal world, especially marine life.

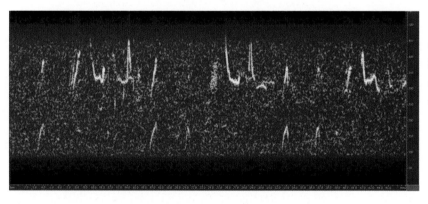

A humpback whale spectrogram is a visual display of the sounds a whale makes.

Since the humpback whale song discovery, other species of whales have been discovered to make sounds, including the endangered blue whale, the largest animal on Earth, as well as bowhead whales. Hydrophones, which are underwater microphones, capture sound in deep water and even beneath ice. Bowhead whales are also on the list of endangered species after nearly being hunted into extinction. Their various melodies are like no other whale, and marine biologists are excited to try to figure out why.

CUSTODIAN OF THE SEA

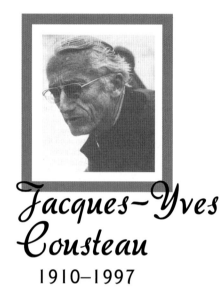

Jacques-Yves Cousteau
1910–1997

Jacques-Yves Cousteau is one of the most famous marine biologists who wasn't even a marine biologist. He was a French naval officer and later an ocean explorer. Jacques Cousteau helped invent the first automatic Aqua Lung, a scuba device that allowed divers to swim underwater for long periods of time. He also helped invent other tools useful to marine biologists and oceanographers, such as underwater cameras. The famous explorer promoted exploring the oceans and the sport of scuba diving. He produced and starred in his own show, *The Undersea World of Jacques Cousteau.* He founded the Cousteau Society in 1973 and dedicated it to marine conservation. Even though the founder is gone, the Cousteau Society continues its efforts to be "custodians of the sea."

The twin-hose Aqua Lung was the first open-circuit free-swimming breathing set for underwater exploration. It was developed by Jacques-Yves Cousteau and Emile Gagnan in 1943.

Quote: *You study dolphins? How cool!* I can't begin to say how many times I've heard this. It seems what I do is something many people dream about. The adventurous, romantic life of a marine biologist, out in the elements, investigating the lives of these magnificent creatures in the freedom of the vast ocean ...

I am fortunate indeed, and I wouldn't exchange my life and career for anything. But people don't often realize what goes into the job. For every hour I log at sea, there are probably at least five to spend in the lab back on land. The work is as long and hard as it's rewarding, both on and off the water, but the many hours passed hunched over a desk as the clock ticks late into the night, analyzing, writing, correcting, rewriting, are where the less committed tend to weed themselves out of the vocation. (Maddalena Bearzi, *Dolphin Confidential: Confessions of a Field Biologist.* Chicago: University Of Chicago Press, 2012)

People depend on our streams, rivers, lakes, and oceans for food, energy, transportation, and health of our **atmosphere**. Marine biologists contribute knowledge about marine life that teaches us how to take care of our valuable resources. Want to get involved?

You can read more books, take science classes, and volunteer for local marine conservation efforts. A lot of a marine biologist's work involves raising money for research projects. With a little creativity, you can help support their research by planning fundraisers with your friends and classmates.

Explore the shorelines, streams, lakes, and rivers around you. Use an identification book to identify the plants and animals you see there. Look under rocks! Take notes and photos and start a journal. Focus on one plant or animal and study it. A small microscope can reveal a miniature world of marine life. Visit a public aquarium. Raise sea creatures in your own aquarium. It's an exciting world to explore!

CITIZEN SCIENTIST

Glossary

acoustic (uh-KOO-stik): to do with sound or hearing

atmosphere (AT-muhss-fihr): the mixture of gasses that surrounds a planet

bioactive (bi-o-ACT-iv): having an effect on a living organism

conservation (kon-sur-VAY-shuhn): the protection of valuable things, especially natural resources

ecosystems (EK-oh-siss-tuhmz): communities of animals and plants interacting with the environment

estuaries (ESS-chu-er-eez): the wide part of a river where it joins the sea

hydroelectric (hye-droh-i-LEK-trik): to do with production of electricity using water

oceanography (oh-shuh-NOG-ruh-fee): the science that deals with the oceans and the plants and animals that live in them

organisms (or-guh-NIZ-uhmz): living plants or animals

spawn (SPAWN): to produce a large number of eggs

tributaries (trib-yuh-ter-ees): rivers or streams flowing into larger streams or rivers

watershed (WAW-tur-shed): the region that drains into a river or lake

Index

Show What You Know

1. How do marine biologists know how far some leatherback turtles travel in the ocean?

2. What is a bioactive compound? How do marine biologists relate to them?

3. Why are sea otters important?

4. What types of information does a marine biologist record?

5. What are some reasons fish become threatened or endangered?

Websites to Visit

www.marinebio.org/marinebio/games

www.kids.earth.nasa.gov/archive/career/oceanographer.html

www.marinebio.org/news/#mb

About the Author

Robin Koontz is a freelance author/illustrator/designer of a wide variety of nonfiction and fiction books, educational blogs, and magazine articles for children and young adults. Her 2011 science title, *"Leaps and Creeps - How Animals Move to Survive,"* was an Animal Behavior Society Outstanding Children's Book Award Finalist. Raised in Maryland and Alabama, Robin now lives with her husband in the Coast Range of western Oregon where she especially enjoys observing the wildlife on her property. You can learn more on her blog, robinkoontz.wordpress.com.

Meet The Author!
www.meetREMauthors.com

www.rourkeeducationalmedia.com

PHOTO CREDITS: Cover: scuba diver photo © frantisekhojdysz, whaleshark photo © davidpstephens; page 4-5 © masked; map page 4 © Olinchuk; page 6 © Lynsey Allan; page 7 paper © CGinspiration, water droplets © 31moonlight31, green turtle © LauraD, hawksbill turtle © NaturePhoto, Kemps Ridley turtle © Evgeniapp, leatherback © IrinaK, loggerhead © Polly Dawson, olive ridley turtle © Joost van Uffelen; page 8 map © Olinchuk, leatherback © IrinaK, satellite © bluebay, page 9 © jellyfish © Boris Pamikov; page 10 © IrinaK; page 11 © © seegraswiese; page 12 © frantisekhojdysz; PAGE 13 courtesy of NASA; page 14 © Marinerock, MidoSemsem; page 15 © Georgios Kollidas, Nicku; page 16 © Stefan Pircher; page 17 top © Tui-PhotoEngineer, bottom © NOAA; page 18-19 courtesy of Robert Schwemmer, CINMS, NOAA, page 19 courtesy of NOAA; page 20 map © pavalena, page 20-21 © Richard Whitcombe; page 22-23 © davidpstephens; page 25 © Sarah_Ackerman http://www.flickr.com/photos/sackerman519/4251357083/; Page 26-27 © Terence, page 27 courtesy of Tania Larson, USGS.; page 28 © Marcos Amend, page 28 map USGS, page 28-29 © worldswildlifewonders; page 30 © Jean-Edouard Rozey; page 31 kelp © Antonia Lorenzo, urchin © NatalieJean; page 32 map © AridOcean, map of U.S. © Prospective56, page 33 top courtesy of U.S. Geological Survey/photo by Tom Roorda, page 34 photo by Larry Ward, Lower Elwha Fisheries Office; page 35 top courtesy of U.S. Geological Survey/photo by Jeff Duda, bottom courtesy of U.S. Geological Survey/photo by Ian Miller; page 36 courtesy of U.S. Geological Survey/photo by Chris Magirl, page 37 courtesy of U.S. Geological Survey/photo by John Felis; page 38 © Valeriy Kirsanov; page 39 courtesy of the National Park Service; page 40-41 © Ethan Daniels, inset photo © NOAA; page 42 © NOAA, page 43 Cousteau photo courtesy of NASA, bottom photo © aqualung © Anthony Appleyard at the wikipedia project; page 45 logo © maximillion1, photo © Imfoto

Edited by: Keli Sipperley

Cover and Interior design by: Nicola Stratford   www.nicolastratford.com

Library of Congress PCN Data

Marine Biologists / Robin Koontz
(Scientists in the Field)
ISBN 978-1-63430-408-5 (hard cover)
ISBN 978-1-63430-508-2 (soft cover)
ISBN 978-1-63430-600-3 (e-Book)
Library of Congress Control Number: 2015931704

Also Available as: